CONTENTS

13 CHECK OUT THE TOP 10 iG ACCOUNTS

Photo Credit: @nataliemeleka via weheartit

09
MOST VIEWED iG VIDEO!

You will not want to miss this. And it is not from your average celebrity or your typical influencer. We still do not know how it got to 350M VIEWS!

11
WHERE IS THE EGG?

A few months ago the EGG broke iG with the most liked picture of ALL TIME! Check out the latest updates on the EGG and where it is headed.

 MEDIA@IGMONTHLY.COM

 @IGMONTHLY

 WWW.IGMONTHLY.COM

01

Photo Credit Cover: Bronny James via @bronny on Instagram, Pogba Getty Images

best iG captions.

Mom: Why is everything on the floor? Me: Gravity!

TOP 10 INFLUENCERS
of our time by iGMonthly

10

GENRE: SPORTS   **SÉAN GARNIER**

seanfreestyle ✓   Follow

3,993 posts   **3.3m** followers   **1,210** following

Séan Garnier
2X World Champion 🏆🏆
3X France Champion 🏆🏆🏆
REDBULL ATHLETE
Paris - Dubai 📍
@URBANBALL

Séan Garnier is considered one of the best freestylers in the world and has also won the French Freestyle and the Styllball Beach Style. He got his start as a competitive soccer player for clubs like Troyes and Auxerre.

iG WITHOUT LIKES

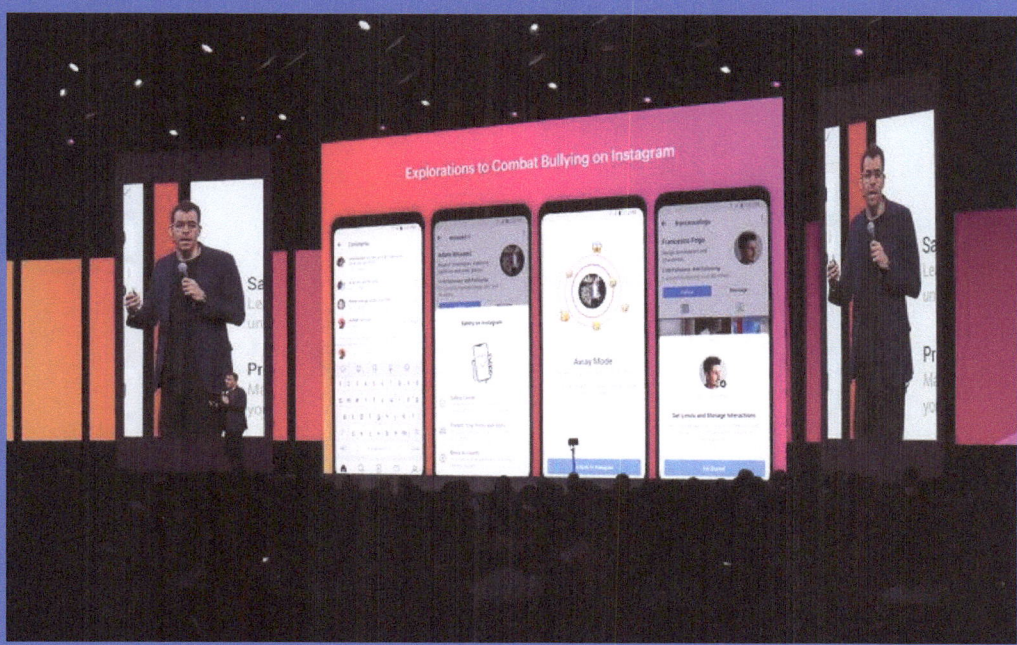

Instagram head Adam Mosseri introduces new changes to Instagram, including a test to "hide" likes for Canadian users. Photo Credit: Justin Sullivan via Getty Images

Given Instagram's recent increased efforts to prioritize mental health — Instagram Stories were created in part to alleviate the pressure of receiving likes — the test makes a lot of sense. At F8, Mosseri said that this feature was set up in order to create a "less pressurized environment where people feel comfortable expressing themselves." (Likes can also create a false sense of engagement, given the number of bots and services that exist to send fake likes to posts.)

Even better for Instagram's bottom line — i.e time spent on site — Canadians we spoke to said they're posting more, without the built-up anxiety they used to feel about how the post would perform.

Testing a Change to How You See Likes

We want your followers to focus on what you share, not how many likes your posts get. During this test, only you will be able to see the total number of likes on your posts.

OK

Photo Credit: @gosainnn via Twitter

best iG captions.

Sure, I do marathons. On Netflix.

9

 **TOP 10 INFLUENCERS**
of our time by iGMonthly

GENRE: MEDICAL   **DR. MIKE VARSHAVSKI**

doctor.mike ✔️ [Follow]

614 posts   **3.1m** followers   **202** following

Dr. Mike Varshavski
Board Certified FM Physician NYC 🩺🚑
Avid Explorer of Life & Dog Dad 🐶🌍
📍 DoctorMikeMedia@gmail.com
THIS IS MY ONLY IG ACCOUNT! YouTube ✌️👇
goo.gl/pakoGu

Mikhail Varshavski, Doctor Mike, is a third-year family medical resident at Overlook Medical Center focusing on family and preventative medicine. A Buzzfeed article in mid-2015 described Doctor Mike as "the hottest man on Instagram", and in November that year People magazine named him the "Sexiest Doctor Alive".

INSTAWARS

DRAKE X MALLORY EDENS

@ @champagnepapi

57M
Followers

1,942
Following

@mallory_edens @

200k
Followers

431
Following

The 6God typically isn't one to shy away from social media altercation, so when Mallory Edens – the daughter of Milwaukee Bucks owner Wes Edens – trolled Drizzy by wearing a shirt with the image of Pusha T (Pusha tee?) during Game Five of the Eastern Conference Finals of the 2019 NBA Playoffs, Drake hit back in typical Drake fashion. The Raptors went on to win the game, and you can see the shirt in question below.

Photo Credit: Getty Images

In a now deleted post, the Raptors ambassador posted an image of Edens in his Instagram story with the caption "All is fair in war and war and trust me I'll still get you tickets to ovo fest." He then went one step further changing his Instagram profile picture to a photograph of Edens.

Now trending, Mallory grew over 100k followers instantly and is now at over 200k.

Credit: HighsNobiety, Read More: http://bit.ly/2WsX30q

best iG captions.

Did it for the memories – totally worth it!

8

 **TOP 10 INFLUENCERS**
of our time by iGMonthly

GENRE: DESIGN   **JOANNA GAINES**

 **joannagaines** ✓ [Follow]

2,100 posts   10.8m followers   451 following

Joanna Stevens Gaines
Wife. Mama. Designer. Shop owner. Homebody. Chk out our magazine #MagnoliaJournal. Follow @magnolia for our shop updates!
magno.li/chipin

Joanna Gaines is known for being a host on HGTV's Fixer Upper. This show allows her to show off the renovations that she and her husband, Chip, have done as owners of renovation business, Magnolia Homes. While Chip has the real estate knowledge and experience, Joanna brings design flair to the team.

NEW TO IG

New!

BRONNY JAMES JOINS INSTAGRAM

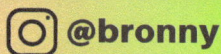
@bronny

1.9M
Followers

163
Following

Bronny James, Lebron James's Son, joins instagram under the handle @real_bronny, which he later changed to @bronny. Lebron James helped boost his sons popularity by sharing his profile in one of his posts. Bronny saw an instant increase in followers, reaching a million followers in less than a day.

Bronny James is a rising Class of 2023 prospect who will be a freshman next season at Sierra Canyon, a California powerhouse high school program that perennially produces college talent.

best iG captions.

Do I run? Yes... Out of time, patience and money.

7

TOP 10 INFLUENCERS
of our time by iGMonthly

GENRE: TRAVEL   **JAY ALVARREZ**

jayalvarrez ✔   [Follow]

556 posts   **6.5m** followers   **878** following

JAY ALVARREZ
Free Spirit 💗 Love is #1
OMERTÀ CORTEX
Teamjay@mail.com
My Jewelry collection ↩
savageisle.com

Jay Alvarrez is a model, who was born and grew up in Hawaii. He loves surfing and the outdoor life, and his Instagram posts certainly reflect this. Many of his posts show him surfing or engaged in some form of daredevil activity, such as skydiving. He is probably best known for documenting his travel and extreme sports activities

iG Fun Fact

NOT YOUR TYPICAL CELEBRITY

MOST VIEWED VIDEO OF ALL TIME!

⟲ @letterlapse

73k
Followers

1,358
Following

350M
VIEWS

The most viewed video on instragam is a time lapsed drawing by @letterlapse. We verified it and it actually is true. Though we can not explain how they did it, the video has over 350 Million views on Instagram, surpassing other celebrity videos by Kylie Jenner and Kim Kardashian.

best iG captions.

There's no "we" in fries

6

TOP 10 INFLUENCERS
of our time by iGMonthly

GENRE: FASHION   **CHIARA FERRAGNI**

chiaraferragni ✔ [Follow]

12,762 posts   **16.7m** followers   **967** following

Chiara Ferragni
Love fiercely (and don't forget to stop along the way to take photos) Founder of @chiaraferragnicollection, @theblondesalad and @beautybites
www.douglas.it/index_b011460.html

Chiara Ferragni is an Italian-born, but New York-based, blogger and fashion designer. She has worked for Guess as a model and spokesperson. She runs a fashion blog named The Blonde Salad and her Instagram postings are an offshoot of that.

Where is the EGG

@world_record_egg

8.6M
Followers

927
Following

It looks like the creators of the World Record EGG are turning our friend into a character. The most recent posts show the EGG doing workouts and exercise. We saw in April various promotions from Dj Khaled and the Jonas Brothers on the instagram account page of the EGG, @world_record_egg.

Fun Fact

@world_record_egg holds the record for instagram's most liked photo with 53M Likes!

11

best iG captions.

I know the voices in my head aren't real..... but sometimes their ideas are just absolutely awesome!

5

 ## TOP 10 INFLUENCERS
of our time by iGMonthly

GENRE: FITNESS   **MICHELLE LEWIN**

michelle_lewin ✓ **Follow**

1,416 posts   13.4m followers   222 following

Michelle Lewin
#lacuerpa - Here to motivate AF
My Gym Wear: @one0one_101
My Street Wear: @m.elle.store
My Workout Plans: @fitplan_app
My Meal Plans: @mealplan_app

Initially a Venezuelan model, Michelle Lewin is a South Florida-based star of the fitness world. She increases her followers across all of her social media channels by an astounding 20,000 per day.

TOP 10 ON iG

TAYLOR SWIFT

10

@taylorswift

118M
Followers

0
Following

Taylor Swift is an amazing songwriter and world's leading contemporary recording artists. She does not share as open picture as Kim Kardashian and Beyonce on Instagram. Taylor has been sharing some cryptic clues about what we think might be some new music on the way. Notably, she is one of twelve women who has been featured in Time's 100 most influential people in the world at least three times (2010, 2015, 2019). Taylor Swift has more than 115 million followers on Instagram and but does not follow a single person on the photo-video sharing application.

MAY iG Highlights

Most Liked

2.2M
Likes

Most Viewed

3.1M
Views

13

best iG captions.

Going to bed early. Not going to a party. Not leaving my house. My childhood punishments has become my adult goals.

(4)

 **TOP 10 INFLUENCERS**
of our time by iGMonthly

GENRE: ENTREPRENEUR   **TAI LOPEZ**

tailopez ✓   Follow

2,156 posts   3m followers   7,344 following

Tai Lopez
🚗 I give away cash, cars, & laptops. 475 won so far: 10 cars, 540 cash & prize winners
Investor/Philanthropist/Mensa
Read 1 book/day
10M TedX

Tai Lopez works with over 20 multi-million dollar businesses as an investor, partner, consultant, and advisor. He uses the internet to help motivate businesses and people towards financial success. This includes operating a book club with a Book of the Day email and producing podcasts.

TOP 10 ON iG

NEYMAR JR

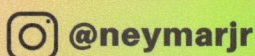
@neymarjr

119M
Followers

1,025
Following

Neymar is a Brazillian football player, who currently plays as a forward for French club Paris Saint-Germain and the Brazil national team. He is regarded as one of the best players in the world. He is popularly known for his dribbling, finishing, skill, pace, and ability to play with both feet. in 2018, Neymar was listed by Time to be one of the most influential people in the world. France Football ranked him as the world's third highest paid footballer, whose estimated earning is €81.5m ($95m) for a calendar year in combined income from salaries, bonuses, and endorsements. He Neymar has 114 million followers on Instagram and follows 996 people.

MAY iG Highlights

Most Liked

5.7M Likes

Most Viewed

14.8M Views

15

best iG captions.

They say don't try this at home...so I went to my friends home!

3

 ## TOP 10 INFLUENCERS
of our time by iGMonthly

GENRE: PERSONALITY   **JAKE PAUL**

 jakepaul ✔ [Follow]

936 posts   11.9m followers   650 following

Jake Paul
new music video "i'm single" OUT NOW 👌 👌
youtu.be/1g1drZ1j-C0

His specialty is making comedy videos. Although he does have some videos on Instagram, most of his images appear to be shots of him going about his everyday life, including posing with a few fans. Jake has recently launched TeamDom, an influencer marketing management and creative agency.

TOP 10 ON iG

LEONEL MESSI

8

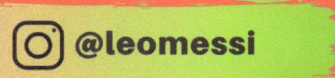
@leomessi

121M
Followers

222
Following

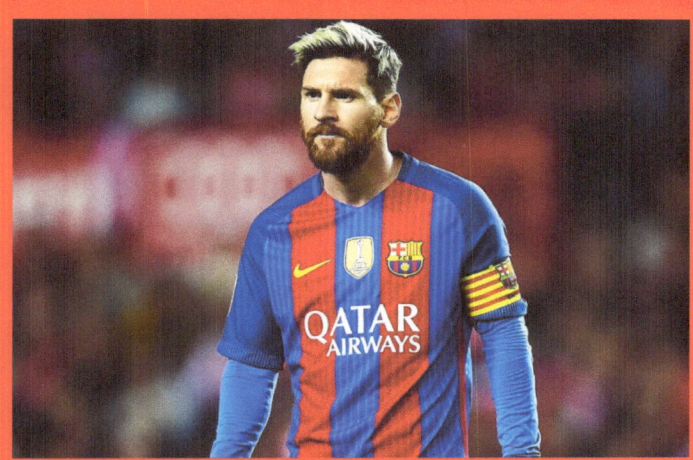

Lionel Messi is an Argentine football player, who currently plays as a forward and captains both Spanish club Barcelona and the Argentina national team. He was born and raised in central Argentina. Messi was diagnosed with a growth hormone deficiency as a child. When he was 13, he relocated to Spain to join Barcelona, who agreed to pay for his medical treatment. He once announced his retirement from international football, but a wave of huge fan support ultimately led him to return to the field.

MAY iG Highlights

Most Liked

9.5M
Likes

Most Viewed

5.9M
Views

best iG captions.

They say: Do what you love and the money will come to you. Just ordered pizza, now I am waiting...

2

 **TOP 10 INFLUENCERS**
of our time by iGMonthly

GENRE: FILMMAKER   **ZACH KING**

 **zachking** ✔ [Follow]

844 posts   **20.3m** followers   **60** following

Zach King
😃 Stories can make people smile.
 12340 Seal Beach Blvd Unit 209
Seal Beach, CA 90740
Contact - hello@zachkingteam.com

Zach King is another film-maker and personality who found fame on the internet. Considering that he is a filmmaker, it is no surprise that most of Zach's Instagram postings are videos.

TOP 10 ON iG

BEYONCÉ

7

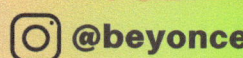

128M
Followers

0
Following

Beyonce is also an American singer, writer and dancer, who has been taking part in singing and dancing competition since her childhood. She earned recognition in late 1990 as the lead singer of the R&B girl-group Destiny's Child. Mathex Knowles, a group managed by her father became one of the best-selling girl groups in history. Her Instagram account is filled with pictures of her performances and the latest photoshoots with her fans. Forbes named her as the most powerful female in entertainment on their 2015 and 2017 lists. She also occupied the sixth place for Time's Person of the Year in 2016. Beyonce's Instagram followers are 127 million but she does not follow a single people.

MAY iG Highlights

Most Liked

Most Viewed

3.7M Likes

20.4M Views

19

best iG captions.

When nothing goes right, go left.

1

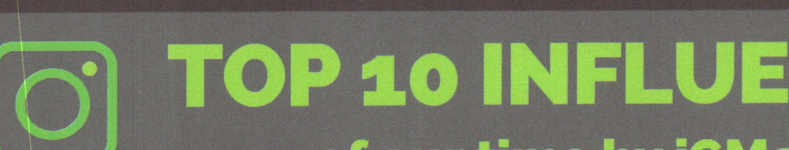

TOP 10 INFLUENCERS
of our time by iGMonthly

GENRE: BEAUTY   **HUDA KATTAN**

hudabeauty ✔   Follow

14,248 posts   **37.6m** followers   **575** following

Huda Kattan
Love my InstaFam 🤗
PROVING DREAMERS
CAN MAKE IT 🙏
Personal Page 👉 @huda
MUA & Blogger, turned Business Woman

Huda is very strong at showing makeup trends, reviews and how-tos. She mixes static images and video in her Instagram feed. She is a businesswoman herself and has her own range of makeup.

TOP 10 ON iG

KYLIE JENNER

6

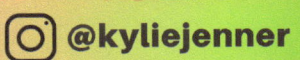
@kyliejenner

137M
Followers

127
Following

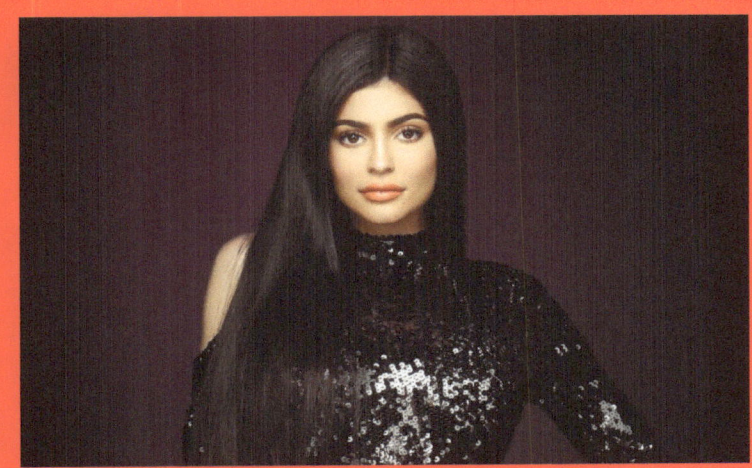

Kylie is an avid social media user, who keeps sharing beautiful photos of her on Instagram. She might not have as a follower as her sister Kim, but she is no less than that. Her makeup brand's account even has more than 20 million followers. Jenner's net worth is estimated at US$1 billion, making her, at age 21, the world's youngest billionaire as of March 2019, reported Forbes. In November 2018, New York Post credited her for being the most influential star in the fashion industry. Kylie Jenner has 132 million followers on Instagram while she follows only 127 people.

MAY iG Highlights

Most Liked

9.4M
Likes

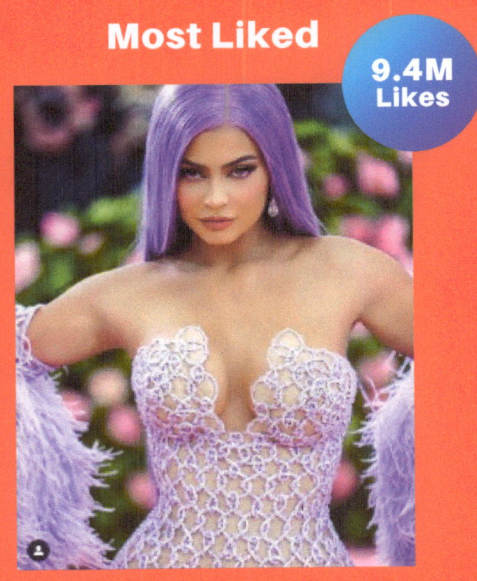

Most Viewed

34.9M
Views

Maybe if we tell people the brain is an app, they will start using it.

715k
Followers

828
Following

@chuckliddell

Chuck "The Iceman" Liddell

Believe it or not, certified knockout artist Chuck Liddell is also a certified accountant. In 1995, Chuck Liddell graduated from California Polytechnic State University with a Bachelor of Arts in Business and Accounting. So much for the stereotype that all accountants are pencil pushing nerds.

Photo Credit: AKA Thailand

Credit: Bleacher Report. Read More: http://bit.ly/2Rew8QP

22

TOP 10 ON iG

KIM KARDASHIAN

5

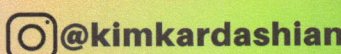
@kimkardashian

141M
Followers

114
Following

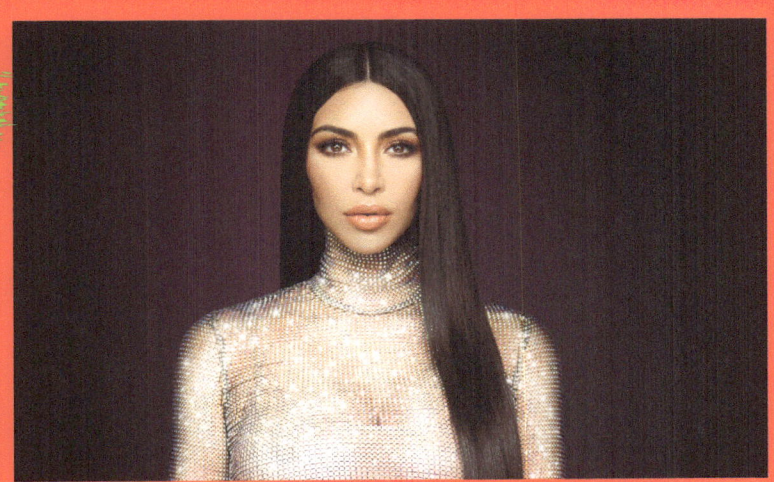

Kim Kardashian is also an American woman, model and businesswoman, who first rose to fame as friend and stylist of Paris Hilton. She was widely covered after a sex tape of her and her boyfriend Ray J was leaked in 2007. She was also named in 100 most influential people in 2015, while Vogue described her a pop culture phenomenon in 2016. She was reported to be the highest-paid reality television personality of 2015, with her total earnings exceeding US$53 million. Kim Kardashian has 135 million followers on Instagram. She only follows 127 people on the photo-video sharing application.

MAY iG Highlights

Most Liked

6.5M
Likes

Most Viewed

21.7M
Views

best iG captions.

For me, math class is like watching a foreign movie without subtitles.

iGMonthly's
Did YOU know

2.4M
Followers

95
Following

@leticiabufoni

Leticia Bufoni

Photo Credit: www.goskate.com

Leticia Bufoni is a four time winner of the World Cup Female Street Skate Championship and a three time gold medalist at the X Games. She began skating at the age of 9 with a group of boys. Her father broke her board in attempt to get her to stop skating with them. He later would take her to her first competition.

TOP 10 ON iG

DWAYNE "THE ROCK" JOHNSON

4

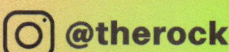 @therock

145M
Followers

370
Following

The retired WWF wrestler and American actor and producer Dwayne Johnson is known for sharing his work out videos and pictures on Instagram. He keeps posting motivational quotes and caption, which gives his fans much-needed positivity every day. Johnson made his acting debut with The Scorpion King (2002) and went on to star in numerous other films, including The Rundown (2003), The Other Guys (2010), Moana (2016), and Jumanji: Welcome to the Jungle (2017). Now, he is one of the highest paid actors in the world. He also managed to induct his name in TIME's 100 Most Influential People in the World list in both 2016 and 2019. The Rock follows 360 people on and is followed by 139 million.

MAY iG Highlights

Most Liked

6.8M
Likes

Most Viewed

23.8M
Views

best iG captions.

Chocolate doesn't ask silly questions, chocolate understands – just like best friends!

 **iGMonthly's Did YOU know**

 **311k** Followers

1,328 Following

 @paolongoria

Paola Longoria

Photo Credit: www.listal.com

Women's racquetball player from Mexico who is considered a pioneer in the sport. She was named as one of the 50 Most Influential Women in Mexico by Forbes Magazine in 2013. Her friends call her "Peke" (Little One) because of her 1.64 (under 5'4") height.

TOP 10 ON iG

SELENA GOMEZ

3

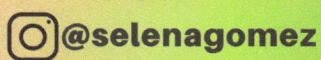
@selenagomez

151M
Followers

59
Following

The second woman in the list is also a singer-writer and musician, Selena Gomez. After working on the children's television series titled Barney & Friends, she rose to fame for her role portrayal of Alex Russo on the Disney Channel television series Wizards of Waverly Place, which aired for four seasons from 2007 until 2012. It is to be noted that she used to be the most followed woman on Instagram but it has been taken by Ariana Grande now. Selena Gomes follows only 59 people on and is followed by 149 million people on Instagram.

MAY iG Highlights

Most Liked

11.7M
Likes

Most Viewed

10.8M
Views

27

best iG captions.

Be happy, it drives people crazy.

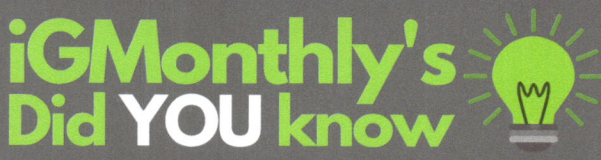
iGMonthly's Did YOU know

1.8M Followers

1,077 Following

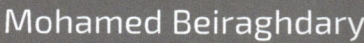
@mo_vlogs_

Mohamed Beiraghdary

Photo Credit: Esquire Middle East

Mo Vlogs is a vlogger and gamer who found success with his YouTube channel 'Mo Vlogs'. Mo's videos on most expensive cars in Dubai earned him immense fame and popularity. Mo's journey into social media started with his gaming channel HitspecK0, but vlogging is where he landed.

TOP 10 ON iG

ARIANA GRANDE

2

@arianagrande

156M
Followers

787
Following

Ariana Grande is one of the biggest and leading contemporary recording artists, who has received multiple accolades, including one Grammy Award, one Brit Award and three American Music Awards. Grande started her career in 2008 in the Broadway musical and earned recognition for her role as Cat Valentine in the Nickelodeon television series. Ariana Grade follows 778 people and being followed by 152 million on Instagram. She has been named as the most followed woman on Instagram in February this year. Time had included her in 100 most influential people in the world in 2016 and 2019.

MAY iG Highlights

Most Liked

6.6M
Likes

Most Viewed

12.1M
Views

29

Credit: THE LIVE MIRROR, Read More: http://bit.ly/2HXSHpG

best iG captions.

You never know what you have until you have cleaned your house.

iGMonthly's Did YOU know

1.6M
Followers

1,019
Following

@rsbelhasa

Rashed Belhasa

He is best known as Money Kicks, and entrepreneur of the clothing brand, who is famous for his exotic collections and vlogging. His shoe and watches collection is no less than a shopping centre. His "Sneaker Talk" series features celebrities like Wiz Khalifa, Tyga, The Game, Silento, Kid Ink, etc.

Photo Credit: Arabian Business

TOP 10 ON iG

CRISTIANO RONALDO

1

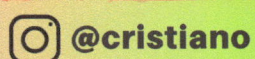

@cristiano

169M
Followers

438
Following

Cristiano Ronaldo is undoubtedly one of the world's best football players in the world. He is regarded as one of the greatest players of all time. Ronaldo currently plays for Juventus F. C and he is also the captain of the Portugal National Team. Apart from the field, he is also one of the most followed football players and celebrities on Instagram. Ronaldo is the first player who has won four European Golden Shoes. Cristiano Ronaldo is being followed by 163 million people on Instagram but he only follows 433 people including Beyonce.

MAY iG Highlights

Most Liked

8.6M
Likes

Most Viewed

47.2M
Views

31

Better an Oooops, than a what if.

 Did **YOU** know

452k Followers

605 Following

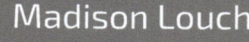

@madds

Madison Louch

Photo Credit: SA Sports Blog

Model and social media sensation. Some of her likes include animals, music, modeling, food, coffee, beach, and anything black and laced. If she could do only one sport her choice would be surfing all the way. When in kindergarden, she learned how to skateboard and dirt bike.

BALLER$ ON VACAY

Air Drake: $200 Million Mega Private Jet

Drake took his $200 Million Private Jet to Turks and Caicos for its first flight. Urban Islandz reported last week that Drake now owns his own private plane dubbed Air Drake, which is a Boeing 767 customized with two bedrooms and loads of other amenities.

Photo Credit: Backgrid

TYGA spotted with Kylie Jenner lookalike

Last month, the "Taste" rapper was spotted on vacation in Montego Bay, Jamaica with a mystery female who looks like his ex-girlfriend Kylie Jenner. Tyga was again spotted out in Los Angeles this week with another Kylie look-a-like on Rodeo Drive.

Pogba flys to the UAE out of the Spotlight

Paul Pogba enjoys downtime in Dubai with girlfriend Maria Salaues as doubts remain over his Manchester United future. The Manchester United midfielder is currently enjoying his end of season break and the couple highlighted their trip on Instagram as they relaxed in the UAE. Pogba has been the subject of speculation linking him to a move to Real Madrid.

best iG captions.

If you were looking for a sign, here it is.

iGMonthly's Did **YOU** know

Natalia Garibotto

Instagram model and social media sensation who has earned more than 1 million followers posting selfies. She studied business law at the University of Miami. She was formerly renowned for her relationship with Cleveland Cavaliers basketball player Kyrie Irving.

Photo Credit: @nataagataa via instagram

iG UPDATES

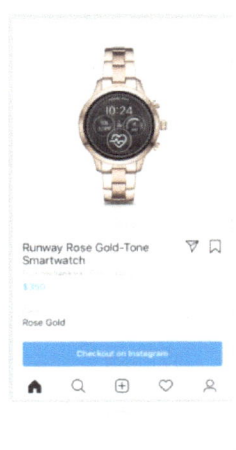
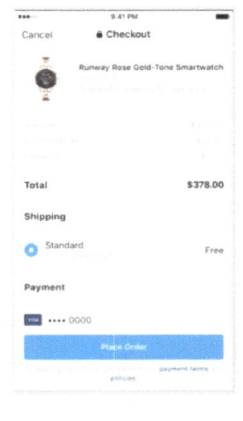

Product Tagging

Creators will be able to Tag Products from other brands. Instagram is currently beta-testing an in-app checkout. This would be a game changer for brands working with influencers to drive sales.

Donation Stickers for Stories

This month, Instagram users in the US are now able to raise money for nonprofits with donation stickers. Users can add these stickers to their profile

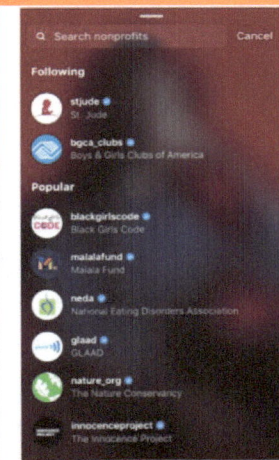

Quiz Stickers

Quiz stickers are the latest addition to the Stories feature, which allow brands and businesses to ask their followers multiple choice questions and provide answers.

???

35

follow us

 **@iGMonthly**